WHAT **WORKS** IN TRANSITION & REENTRY

A Christian Guide to Reducing Recidivism & Victimization

BY JEFF WITT

What Works in Transition and Reentry: A Christian Guide to Reducing Recidivism & Victimization

Trilogy Christian Publishers
A Wholly Owned Subsidary of Trinity Broadcasting Network
2442 Michelle Drive, Tustin, CA 92780

For information, address Trilogy Christian Publishing Rights Department, 2442 Michelle Drive, Tustin, CA 92780.

Trilogy Christian Publishing/TBN and colophon are trademarks of Trinity Broadcasting Network.

For information about special discounts for bulk purchases, please contact Trilogy Christian Publishing.

Manufactured in the United States of America

Trilogy Disclaimer: The views and content expressed in this book are those of the author and may not necessarily reflect the views and doctrine of Trilogy Christian Publishing or the Trinity Broadcasting Network.

10 9 8 7 6 5 4 3 2 1
Library of Congress Cataloging-in-Publication Data is available.

ISBN: 978-1-68556-113-0
ISBN: 978-1-68556-114-7 (eBook)

TABLE OF CONTENTS

EXPERT RECOMMENDATIONS

Inmates confined in prison go through many challenges in being forced to conform to schedules and activities imposed upon them that often do not contribute to meeting their own needs or interest. They are told when to wake up in the mornings, what clothes to wear, when they are to eat their meals, what jobs they must report to, when to go to bed at night, etc. When they are released from prison, they must re-adjust to making their own decisions and finding employment themselves and in making wise decisions about budgeting their time, funds, and relationships.

Reentry and transition services do much to help rebuild productive lifestyles and making worthy decisions. Often there are needs for clothing, housing, transportation, worship, and socialization. Rev. Jeff Witt of Prisoners of Christ has prepared helpful information for establishing and maintaining a successful reentry and transition service from a Christian perspective. II Corinthians 5:17 reminds us that believers are forgiven of past sins and failures and become new creatures in Christ with confidence of God's sustaining love and mercy and unlimited resources to face new challenges with renewed hearts and attitudes.

— Rev. Steve McCollum, Chaplain,
New River Correctional Institution and Work Camp,
Florida Department of Corrections

Having led, volunteered, and served in several prison facilities in Northeast Florida, I have seen firsthand the difference Christ has made with incarcerated men who have had a truly repentant heart and choose to serve Christ and not self. This is why I highly recommend Prisoners of Christ in Jacksonville, FL for men transitioning out of prison. POC offers Christ centered programs of mentoring and discipling the men along with job placement and housing programs. Having this focus on Christ sets the men up for success in today's fast paced society. Hearts are changed, and families are rebuilt around serving Christ, community and others.

— Steve Hyrne
Prisoner Fellowship prison ministry
Region 2 Lead North Florida

ALUMNI COMMENTS

My name is Steve, and I was a client and resident leader at Prisoners of Christ from 2016 until 2020. I was born in Michigan but raised in Florida in a good Christian home, chose to hang around the wrong people and do the wrong things which led to my first and only arrest for first degree felony murder and burglary with assault at the age of sixteen (in 1983) and was subsequently given two life sentences, one with a mandatory twenty-five years before being eligible for parole. I continued to live as though I had no hope, and nothing would ever change for the first fifteen years of my incarceration and then I gave my life to Christ. I was unanimously paroled December 13th, 2013, and lived in Tampa and Fort Lauderdale until making my way to Prisoners of Christ in Jacksonville in 2016.

When I came to Prisoners of Christ, I was still trying to figure out how to live as an adult in a free society, something which I had never done because of my age when I went to prison. Prisoners of Christ helped me understand how to do that, I believe with all my heart that it was due to the faith-based nature of the program and it being very structured. All of which reinforced the importance of my relationship with Christ. In 2020 I moved out and have rented my own place, I have a full-time job and a great church family along with my natural family, this has definitely been a journey but I am so incredibly blessed, and a big part of the reason why I am where I am today is because of my relationship with Christ, with my family, and with Prisoners of Christ.

— Steve Medlin

My name is Jackie Cogdell. My successful reentry and transition into society happened because the condition of my heart changed! Having Jesus Christ as the center of my life was and is the best motivation for me to live my best life. I don't live for myself anymore, but I live to please God who died for me (2 Corinthians 5:14,15)! That I could live life more abundantly (John 10:10)! I live to bring glory, honor, and praise to God (Matthew 5:16)! I wanted to be an example for others with a life sentence in prison that it is possible to be released and live a wonderful life. However, Jesus must be the center of their life!

I have experienced struggles since being released from prison yet knowing that I can accomplish all things through Christ who strengthens me (Philippians 4:13)! When trials and struggles came my faith, trust and belief in God is what kept me focused on the goals that I had set for my wife and I to accomplish. We made plans to achieve those goals, but with God first in our lives. We have obtained many of the goals we set for ourselves. Looking forward to the future we are setting more goals we would like to accomplish, but God is still at the center of our lives. Being obedient, faithful with our tithes and offerings, serving the Church as best we can and treating others as we want to be treated. Life has been so rewarding for my wife and me! We are just thankful to God for His blessings and favor!

— Jackie Cogdell

My best advice is to say when I quit living my life with God in it, I started serving Satan by doing many wrong and bad things to people. As well as losing respect for my own life. Once I was led to God again, by many former degenerates, most who were very close friends, I had a life change. That was bringing Christ back to a prominent place in my life and surrounding myself with like-minded people. I can only thank God for all He has done to bring me out of that dark place and giving me a life of total freedom. Not from prison, but from eternal death from my separation from God.

— John Dancy

My name is Henry. I spent a total of thirty years in prison. Fifteen the first arrest and I don't know how many times I've been arrested. POC helped me to stay focused by making me accountable to the program, it also gave me a safe drug and alcohol-free place to live. Christ has and is changing me slowly; He has changed my thinking and attitude about life and Himself. I have a great job, nice truck, my credit score is terrific, I tithe faithfully and give and serve in many different ministries. I am truly a new creation in Christ Jesus.

— Henry Mack

After being in a Transition Program at Everglades Correctional Institution over two years I knew I needed to continue in a structural setting upon my release. So, my mind was made up I would reach out to some transitional programs before being released to gain acceptance, because (CTP) the Correction Transition Program had taught me how important structure was for anyone incarcerated ten years (a decade) or more. And this program (CTP) targeted inmates who were incarcerated for decades, to help prepare them for release back into society, and a structural environment was essential for reintegration to be successful. A transitional program that would propagate components enabling and encouraging continuous growth. Shedding criminal behavior and thinking, an environment where (Faith in God) was a part of the building process (structure). A place where transformation is encountered, and one can start a new beginning with purpose giving back to the community. So that's why I chose (POC) Prisoners of Christ, an environment of structural setting and principles.

— Greg Seymour

INTRODUCTION

Almost every week I have a person stop by our office and ask about reentry and transition services for ex-offenders. Many wonderful prison ministry volunteers, nonprofit leaders and even public service professionals point them to us and often say "if you want to know how to do it best, go see Prisoners of Christ." I would like to take some small credit for these recommendations, but I cannot. For starters everything that is positive is a grace from God. This grace was manifested in the work of many volunteers and staff prior to me coming on board. Matter of fact, I fully believe God showed magnificent mercy in allowing me the opportunity to serve in a great ministry at a wonderful season.

Reentry and transition were not always a welcomed service. Many people who performed any type of prison ministry directed at the incarcerated or formally incarcerated were viewed as naive, "hug a thug" idealist. More recently the shift has been made where society, by in large has recognized the benefits of healthy reentry services. The proof is in the pudding. If a person does time, they are likely to do time again, unless the recidivism cycle is interrupted. This happens when they are assisted in securing a job, a place to reside and welcomed into a community.

The reduction of recidivism decreases victimization by the diminution of crime. If crime is reduced, taxpayers save money on court cost, incarceration cost and most importantly personal pain and suffering. Not only does the offender experience a true second chance but potential victims are sparred. The benefits of a healthy reentry and transition service for ex-offenders has positive results for all people.

This small writing addresses the most common questions I am asked every time I meet with a person desiring to provide this type of service. It is my hope and prayer that the advice provided in this text helps you in a meaningful way as you think about staring or volunteering in a similar ministry. This text is not academic in nature but practical, this is intentional. My desire is for quick, real-life strategies that can be used immediately. I believe much of the advice translates universally to other ministries, volunteers and staff in church settings, nonprofits, and the public sector. This writing is designed to be read from front to back, however, if you are looking for specific advice in a particular section it can be referenced and hopefully helpful.

This text is written from a Christian perspective. As will be explained later in more detail, this is because the Christian principles work. Even if you ascribe to a different belief system, please objectively view this material, and take what you can from it to better aid the population you serve.

One of the other pieces of advice not addressed in this text revolves around the initial idea or desire to serve in this type of ministry. My advice is generally the same for all people in all types of ministries and service. We do not need to recreate the wheel. Just because you feel you are "led" to help and make a difference does not mean you need to start a new ministry.

Certainly, that may be exactly what needs to happen, but I think many times we should find a place to serve and not waste precious resources starting a duplicate ministry. This of course needs to be a matter of prayer and you must allow the guidance of the Holy Spirit to lead you. But do not lose sight of the goal. If the reason you want to serve is to truly help people, joining an existing group may be the absolute best action you can take.

EXPLANATION OF THE TERM "RECIDIVISM"

Recidivism is a word that is used to describe a cycle of re-offending and being re-arrested. The problem with the word is that it is defined differently by every different agency, nonprofit, and author. There is no standard, clear cut, apples to apples metric in utilization. For example, the Florida Department of Corrections defines recidivism as a re-conviction, within three years that results in a person reentering the Department of Corrections. Most local police/sheriff's offices define recidivism as re arrest of a person in a three-year period.

At a glance, these two definitions do not appear that different; however, they are. Suppose a person is arrested and found innocent, suppose they were found not guilty because the actual criminal was caught. They did not reoffend; therefore, they did not recidivate, however, in the rearrest definition, they are counted in a negative manner. The other side of this dilemma is the re conviction and placement back into a state facility. In Florida, if a person is sentenced to incarceration for a term of one year or less, they remain in the county jail. Therefore, according to the reconviction and placement inside a state prison, no one sentenced to a year or less is counted accurately.

And neither of these metrics address the Violation of Probation scenario where a person may be placed back inside prison or jail, and not have committed another crime, but instead broke community control rules. These rules could be the use of alcohol or breaking curfew. Certainly, a person on community control/probation/parole should abide by set rules, yet they are not truly reoffending if a law has not been broken, and a victim does not exist.

This is why, when I hear a group using the term recidivism, I inquire to their metric for defining recidivism. Nonprofits seeking financial support will gladly share their rate of recidivism based on what shines the best light on their organization. I am not implying they are deceptive, but they are often times avoiding a lengthy explanation that few care to hear. Our own problem with this issue arises every year as we apply for public grants, public officials who are entrusted with looking out for the best interest of taxpayers do not have the time or interest in hearing a long explanation, they simply ask for the rate. They want to know how well your program is functioning.

We have a great rate at reducing recidivism for those who complete our program, unfortunately, if the person joins us for one day and absconds, their chances of reoffending rise. Should that person be calculated into our success or failure rate? They did not receive hardly any benefit from our program; however, they were enrolled. This one-day measurement may seem a bit exaggerated, but it is factual, most of the clients who depart our program unsuccessfully do so with in the first several weeks. We have had more than one, violate their probation withing in two days of release from prison. Their probation officers perform their job, they stop by the houses and sometimes witness newly released individuals participating in harmful violations of their release.

Just remember when some group tells you their recidivism rate, to inquire a bit more deeply to how they define the term. Hopefully, one day soon, we will settle on a universal definition, until then, remember statistics only tell part of the story.

INEQUALITY OF BAIL/BOND

There is a lot of conversation about bail and bond reform, this is good, but a true picture of the dilemma is not always portrayed in the dialogue. Current bail and bond procedures hurt people who have few financial means. If a person has money, bail and bond do not detrimentally affect them in the same way.

A small example of this is when a person of few means is arrested, they may be guilty or innocent, yet if they cannot bail out, they lose their job, are delinquent on car payments, rent and other bills. They usually lose their residence, and their transportation is repossessed, thus their credit is damaged. Say, in two months when they finally have their day in count, they are found innocent, or given time served. They start over at a deficit. This situation lends to the reoffence of the person, or if they were innocent, the new criminal.

Another note, worthy of mentioning, if they go before the judge and he/she declare they can receive a time served sentence if they plead guilty or stay in jail for possibly a year and participate in a formal court trial procedure and possibly receive an innocent judgement, the person is most likely going to opt for the time served verdict. Now and forever more they have a record, which affects many other areas of life in a negative fashion.

Bail and bond do need to be reformed, where risk is mitigated not based on money but on likelihood of future crimes and danger to the community. As it currently stands a petty crime, might result in a $1000.00 bond, that a poor person cannot pay, and a violent crime may have a $500,000.00 bond, that an affluent person can afford. In the current setting the violent rich person can be released and the non-violent petty thief remains incarcerated.

Changing the bail/bond system to focus on releasing non dangerous, non-harmful individuals and keeping custody of the opposite would definitely lower the population inside the county jails, but it would also upset an entire trade of bail bonds services. The restructure would put a lot of people out of business. And even though it all sounds simple, it's not. Defining who is truly a risk is, in itself a dangerous task. The last thing anyone one wants is for someone to get hurt because a quick decision was made.

The bail bond reform discussion has led to other topics that if pursued could lower the number of people incarcerated. Below we will candidly look at this topic.

EXPLANATION OF
"EARLY RELEASE DUE TO MINIMAL CRIME"

Much like bail bond reform with the goal of lowering the incarcerated population, there has been much talk of releasing prisoners that only have drug charges. At a cursory glance this sounds like a great idea and for some people it is a perfect scenario, however, again, statistics only share partial facts.

I am certain there are people currently incarcerated due only to a drug charge, however, I know that is the exception to the norm. During my time as the Classification Officer at a county jail, where I weekly entered the court reports, computations, charges and calculated the gain times for individuals returning from their court hearing for state and county sentences I had the benefit of evaluating the process firsthand. What I witnessed repeatedly was violent charges being dropped and the individual pleading down to a lesser drug charge for a lighter sentence. Why might you ask, would a state's attorney do such a thing? Simple, this action saves taxpayer's millions and frees up the court process which is constantly backed up.

Here is how it works; A person is arrested with multiple charges. Let's say one violent assault, a robbery, grand theft, and possession of cocaine. To convict on these charges would require going to court, selecting a jury, securing copious amounts of evidence, and ensuring witnesses and victims testify. This all takes a lot of energy time and tax dollars, by the way the judge, legal clerks, bailiffs, correction officers, states attorney and the public defender are also being compensated by the taxes paid from citizens. If a guilty verdict is reached the judge usually allows the sentences to be "run concurrent" this means if the violent assault charge receives five years, the robbery receives four years, the grand theft receives two years and the possession of cocaine receives four years, then all charges together, if found guilty equal five years, minus gain time for good behavior. If the public defender, judge, and state's attorney agree, and the charged individual accepts the terms, all charges can be dropped except for the possession of cocaine, and he will receive three-five years.

The possession of cocaine is an easy charge to prove, the person had it on them or not, and in today's system where cameras are becoming normal, it is even easier to prove. The other charges are more difficult to get a conviction on, and they require all the previously mentions work, effort, and money.

So once again, looking simply at statistics we can be fooled. I have listened to many podcasts and public radio interviews where academics stated boldly that we have too many people locked up whose only offense was a drug problem. I think a deeper dig into the truth would paint a different picture. With that said.

Reforming the way things work are never as easy as they appear on a podcast. People who are not emersed in the work probably should do much more homework before they provide advice. Practical knowledge and academics are different. They both have merit, but true knowledge and passion must be linked.

WHO WANTS TO HELP
WITH REENTRY AND TRANSITION?

As you begin to speak with others about reentry and transition of the formally incarcerated, you will quicky find there to be two different types of supporters. I mentioned earlier and will again later, that this type of ministry benefits all people, however, not everyone agrees or desires the same results equally. This is okay, the results remain the same, but it can be very helpful when looking for volunteers, donors, and supporters to allow them to understand better what they find valuable.

I know this feels like manipulation or pandering but it's not. It is simply being a good steward of your time and theirs, it is drawing in the lens to focus specifically on what appeals to the person. Never deceive, never lie but show people why this work is valuable in a way they understand and can relate.

Let me go right to the point. I know some people want to help those who are marginalized, downtrodden and in need of assistance. I also know there are plenty of people who are less interested in helping the previously incarcerated and want more done to prevent future crimes and decrease victimization. The benefits of reentry and transition is that both desires are accomplished at the same time. However, when I speak to a city official who is interested in assisting us, I share more about what I feel they desire. Both outcomes occur, but people generally align ideologically in one camp or the other. My suggestion is, be honest but help them understand in the best way possible.

ESSENTIAL ELEMENT FOR SUCCESS

Reentry and Transition services for ex-offenders are not a new idea. They have been attempted through Federal, State, and County services with differing styles and initiatives. Many tactics, programs and concepts have been employed with varying degrees of success. The one thing that remains constant is the simple fact, that if a person makes a lasting and real change, it is because the person has changed. This sounds a little silly, because of course they changed. But this change is different than what is often evaluated by widely accepted forms of measurement.

Many times, success is gaged by whether a person reoffends in an established time period. Recidivism statistics generally are measured in three-year increments. This is not a great metric; however, some quantitative analysis must exist. This parameter shows that a person may not reoffend in three years or not be caught in that time period. The goal, however, is that they never reoffend.

The change referred to here is not a modification of behavior, although positive behavior is a result. The change referred to must take place in the heart. For a person to be successful their heart must be made new, with new desires, a new attitude, a new outlook on life and a new direction. This means that a reentry service can have the best program available, the best staff at hand and have done all the right stuff at the right times and still be unsuccessful, if the person's heart remains unchanged.

Acknowledging this weakness is important in understanding the key and purpose of meaningful assistance. This means a successful reentry and transition service that truly reduces recidivism does not focus on behavioral change, life skills, substance abuse counseling or employment as its main point and purpose. Instead, the primary success element is a changed heart.

Reentry services that have a lasting impact will have a heart change as their goal, this is why faith-based organizations have greater success rates than programs that primarily focus on behavioral modification. If this concept bothers you, please keep reading anyway. The ideas in this book work. The goal is to change lives for the better. Learning what is successful and what is not successful will prevent futile efforts, assist people experience a flourishing life, reduce crime, and save taxpayers copious amounts of money. Therefore, let us look at the purpose and main point for reentry and transition services.

PURPOSE FOR SERVICES

After pastoring a church for many years, I went to work for the Florida Department of Corrections as an officer. The facility I served at was a maximum-security prison in which most of the inmates had been in trouble in other correctional facilities and were now on what is called Close Management, meaning, they were considered troublemakers. It did not take long for me to realize that most individuals working alongside me thought they were decent good people and those behind the bars were evil. After all they were free, and the others were locked up for varying crimes. Some of the crimes were quite disturbing, the last six months I worked at the prison I spent on Death Row. These initial interactions reminded me of college and some of my areas of study.

During my time in undergraduate school, I focused on Applied Ethics and distinctly remember studying the "Problem of Evil" theory in which we read diary excerpts of Rudolf Hoess, the man in charge of Auschwitz Extermination Camp in Nazi Germany. We also watched videos of the Milgram Experiments and evaluated the My Lai Massacre in Vietnam. We were taught repeatedly that there are no bad people only bad and evil actions. Much like the officer's thoughts about their own virtue, this is an unbiblical and erroneous understanding of the human condition.

The Bible says, "The heart is deceitful above all things, and desperately wicked: who can know it?" Jeremiah 17:9 (KJV). This means that the people on both sides of the bars share the same problem. This means that the villagers in Vietnam had the same problem with God that the soldiers who killed women and children had. This also means that you and I stand in front of God with the same guilt and disgust for our life and actions as the leader of Auschwitz Extermination Camp. We are not good people who make bad choices, we are evil people who act completely directed by our selfish desires. We do nothing altruistically; every leaning for good has a self-serving vein. This is disturbing and unwelcome in most academic settings, people want to be viewed as good people, and again this proves the point. People want to be thought of as good, another self-serving desire.

The positive side of this truth is that all people need help and help is available to all people, no matter what occurred in the past. We must, however, realize our condition as helpless, sinners in the sight of God. This is the central and fundamental point to all healthy mission work; the need for a rescuer, a savior a way to be right in the sight of God. This point is what sets a successful organization apart from a group that tries to help people make better choices. This central truth is exemplified in the Bible and should be shared by word, deed, attitude, and action during all ministry endeavors.

It has been widely reported that the great evangelist D.L. Moody said, "you must get a person lost before you can get them saved." Meaning; that it is essential for a person to understand their need for rescuing before they will seek to be rescued. We have a saying, as we work with people needing real life tangible assistance and it is, "you cannot want it (help) more than they want it (help)." We usually share this saying with a person who is exhausted from trying to offer aid to an individual who really does not want to change their life for the better.

Our goal in ministry is to help people know eternal truth about themselves, their future and what God has planned for them. For their life to change they must first recognize they are lost and need rescuing, Romans 3:23 (KJV) say, "For all have sinned, and come short of the glory of God." They then need to understand that the penalty for that sin is spiritual death, separation from God, "For the wages of sin is death; but the gift of God is eternal life through Jesus Christ our Lord" Romans 6:23 (KJV). The last part of this passage gives hope. Yes, our sin has an eternal penalty, but God in His goodness makes a way for us to have eternal life.

That life is through what Christ did on the Cross as our substitute, 1 John 1:9 (KJV) says, "If we confess our sins, he is faithful and just to forgive us our sins, and to cleanse us from all unrighteousness." This is why we help find jobs and housing, this is why we have mentoring and substance abuse courses. Our goal is for the lost to come to Christ and for the believers to mature in their walk. When this happens, lives change, actions alter, and people become new. Without a genuine heart transplant through the acceptance of Christ as Lord and Savior all the mentoring and life skills classes are pointless. They only provide temporary comfort to people on their path to hell. Mark 8:36 (KJV) "For what shall it profit a man, if he shall gain the whole world, and lose his own soul?"

Many of our clients have a longing and desire to give back. They want to help others come to know Christ as they know Him. They want others to avoid the hard lessons they could have avoided if they had been open to God's plan earlier in life. Because of this desire they are asked often to speak at different events. These engagements have ranged from interdictions, prisons, reentry centers, juvenile detention facilities, support groups and even law enforcement meetings. On one recent occasion at a support group for parents of incarcerated adult children, one of our clients told the mothers that many of their children were right where they needed to be. He said if it had not been for prison, he would be dead like all his friends and would have most likely not called out to God for help. He stated very clearly that it is better to have spent thirty-five years in prison and eternity in heaven than his whole life free and eternity in Hell. When evaluated through the lens of eternity, seemingly negative events in life can have positive results. God is never caught off guard or surprised. We are responsible for our response to His free gift of salvation, which enables sanctification, which is just a fancy word for spiritual maturity.

> "If a brother or sister be naked, and destitute
> of daily food, and one of you say unto them,
> 'Depart in peace, be ye warmed and filled;
> notwithstanding ye give them not those things
> which are needful to the body; what doth it
> profit?' Even so faith, if it hath not works, is
> dead, being alone."
> — James 2:15-17 (KJV)

We strive to share the love, grace, and truth of God's Word and one of the ways we carry this out is through our actions. This leads to the practical outworking of faith.

HOW THE PURPOSE IS EXERCISED

In conjunction with the primary goal of introducing people to Christ we use a twofold focus to re-entry, the first area of concentration is residential, and the second focus is employment. The residential service always overlaps the employment service; however, a client can participate in the employment services without being a resident. Each focus ascribes to a different metric for measuring performance and a different design for executing initiative. The individual designs are as follows:

Residential Services

We accept new clients only through direct application; we do not accept third-party inquires in lieu of personal applications. Our Residential Director responds to potential clients by sending an application, accompanied by a letter describing our program. We request a narrative from the applicant detailing their upbringing, crimes, drug usage history, and future goals. Once the application is received at the office, we send a letter asking for institutional references. These are usually provided by a classification officer, a program facilitator, or a chaplain. After the references are received, a telephone interview is arranged with the classification/release officer and the client. It is during this time that a determination is made to accept or reject the applicant. Acceptance into the program is not based upon the severity of the crime, or the age, nationality, or religious affiliation of the applicant. Our decision is based upon whether the applicant has demonstrated a willingness to participate in our structured program.

New clients are sent a letter confirming their acceptance into the program. Three days prior to their release, a call is made to the classification officer to obtain the clients' bus arrival information. The client is picked up at the bus station by a waiting staff member and taken to the house where he will reside. Depending on his arrival time, he is taken that day or the next to register as a felon and for supervision if applicable. Once registration is complete, he is brought to the office where we determine his need regarding clothing. Each client is provided new underwear, socks, and clothing for work and daily life.

The client then begins an orientation session. An intake assessment helps us understand each client's physical and emotional needs. The client then reads and signs a consent form, reentry services check list, client budget plan, goals sheet, independent living plan, and the residential agreement, which details the house and safety rules for residence. This document also states that the client's participation is voluntary, but as long as he remains in the program, he will comply with all program rules and curriculum requirements. Grievance procedures are explained to the client. The client is then asked to record in writing his immediate and long-term goals. We prepare a case file for the client where all required documentation is housed. We maintain the residential client files physically and digitally for a minimum of five years.

Next, the client receives assistance in filing for food stamps, medical and dental help if needed, and disability and Social Security benefits if eligible. Personal counseling is provided upon request. Guidance is offered regarding obtaining or reinstating driver's licenses. A computer is provided at the office for use by clients who desire to take on-line practice test for a driver's license. The new client is shown how to sign up for an email address and how to obtain a government-issued phone.

The client then moves on to the employment phase. A resume is prepared, and interview skills are taught and practiced, with special attention on how to answer the difficult incarceration related questions during an interview. Job listings are searched, and resumes submitted utilizing our extensive contacts. Interviews are scheduled. Appropriate interview clothes and transportation to the interview are provided.

Each client is on the "buddy system" until they are employed. This means that he will not be allowed to go anywhere alone but will be accompanied by another client with proven stability in the program during this critical time. Once employed, each client begins to pay weekly rent. Clients are required to attend a weekly Substance Abuse Meeting. Depending on their past, they may be required to also attend a 12-step meeting each week. Twice monthly, each client is also required to attend a community meeting, where life skill curriculum is utilized. This is a time when all the men in the residential program come together for dinner and discussion of any problems, changes, or general announcements. It is also a time for men to share good reports and victories. The positive benefits of seeing peers succeeding in transition are helpful to men working to restart their lives. Though not required, clients are encouraged to perform community service.

Clients are monitored through daily interaction, random drug testing, and review of their progress toward their goals in hopes of assuring a successful transition. Post transition housing and budgeting issues are discussed. At three, six, nine and twelve months in the program, we conduct formal interviews with the client to find out how they are progressing toward their plan and goals. Most residential clients transition after being with us for six to nine months. Upon completion of our program, whether successful or unsuccessful, if the client is under supervision, their probation officer is notified.

Bus passes are supplied to new clients, at no cost until after they are employed and receiving pay. All the residential houses are close to bus line routes. Many clients obtain their own transportation shortly after they are employed. Some of our clients continue to take part in the substance abuse and community gatherings after they leave the program. If the client allows, we maintain contact with them following their transition.

We use several innovative paths to help transition ex-felons/returning citizens. Each house has five residents, including four transitioning clients and a house manager. The House Manager is a former client who remains as a House Manager to help guide existing clients through questions and issues that arise in transitioning. The House Manager also serves in an accountability position within the house. He reminds clients, if needed, of the requirement to keep rooms clean, neat, and ready for viewing, house sanitation, personal hygiene matters and the like. The house system is designed to create a home and family atmosphere where clients learn to live together with cooperation and consideration of others. Clients generally share rooms, learning to share space equitably, and resolve normal daily issues, like time in the bathroom and sharing closet space. These actions add to the foundation necessary to successfully live life in today's society.

Employment Services

Clients entering only the jobs program are scheduled for two appointments usually back-to-back on the same day. The first appointment helps the client develop a resume with focus on their individual skills. They are coached how to interact with potential employers and given advice on how to answer difficult questions about their past, honestly. This resume is sent to them electronically for their future use and they are also given several paper copies.

The next appointment is with our employment specialist that focusses on job placement. This is a two-step process.

First the client is assisted with finding an immediate job. Many times, before the client leaves the premises, they have interviews scheduled. We have a positive reputation and relationship with many organizations in the Jacksonville area. Some employers call us looking for potential staff. This first job may or may not be a perfect match; usually a first job helps with bills, but is not the dream job, the dream job generally requires more time in acquiring. We do not find a job and then abandon the client. We also assist them in locating their forever job; the vocation they desire to stay in long term. This is another area that tremendously helps people abstain from re-offending. Once a person has purpose, direction, and a vocation they feel is a calling, they happily devote their energy to that endeavor.

The employment program has two specialist and support staff along with an administrator who divides time between both programs. The residential program has five direct supervisors, one for each home; they reside on the property, one full time residential director over all the homes, support staff and the administrator.

The employment and residential services can become a bit mechanical and regimented if we are not careful to stay close to God's directing. Again, these are support tools to accomplish the sacred action of introducing the lost to Christ. The actions listed above should be used as a way to help people know Christs' love and allow them to witness the incarnation of God through our behavior.

This leads to another important delineation that is problematic in ministry; the clarification of what is supportive and what is sacred. What is a biblical practice and what falls under the category of a preference? It should be easy to decide to follow God's Word and not get sidetracked with personal preferences, but it can become difficult. Especially if we have experienced God moving in a particular way in the past through specific actions, we can link those activities to His desires, when they may have only been a way in which he delivered His message for that particular time and place. This reaches into uncomfortable, church dividing topics like music style, place or time of worship and Bible translations. We must remember the delivery style of the sacred is not the sacred; how we share truth is not truth itself. It is not just faith-based organizations that face this dilemma, all groups must focus on why they exist and when they lose sight of that focus and key reason for their existence they begin to drift away from their mission.

One of the primary problems with losing focus takes place during and through the process of securing means to carry out the mission. Development, fund raising, offerings, charity or however you desire to label the money needed to pay the bills is and will remain a key challenge. It will also become the "tail that often wags the dog" meaning if a group is not careful, they will curtail their practices to cater to those who provide for the work. Often times the funding source has desires or preferences that when met are rewarded with funding and when not met, hold back those needed monetary resources. It can become easy to set aside the primary goal of the organization to keep the organization alive. This is the beginning stages of the death of a ministry. Below we will evaluate a few different sources and discuss what is positive and what is negative about different revenue streams.

FUNDING

Funding is the primary challenge in reentry and transition services. Working with ex-offenders is not an easy topic to raise money for. If you have children you wish to help, or cute little animals, people seem to be more inclined to assist. We could show as many pictures of a person as possible, but it would not motivate the heart and emotions like a photo of a child in need. Financial resources are essential to operations. Having residential services cost a lot with insurance, utilities, upkeep, and maintenance, not to mention staff to oversee the ministry. The employment program must have a designated meeting site, computers, utilities, upkeep, liability, and property insurance cost along with staff that are trained and competent to assist in job placement.

Funding is a constant battle and once you have a year's commitment through private or public grants you will need to begin searching for resources for the next year. Two primary funding sources exist, they are public and private. They are in the forms of gifts, grants, and partnerships. Both public and private funding sources have positive and negatives aspects. Below we will evaluate each with as much objectivity as possible.

BENEFITS AND DRAWBACKS
OF PUBLIC FUNDING

Public funding is a blessing in many ways, primarily because it is steady and dependable. If an organization receives grants or partnership resources from a government agency those resources are generally stable and can be counted upon. Of course, we have experienced government shutdowns in the past and resources can be "frozen," but they are paid once normal operations resume. The funding may end but it ends once the agreed grant has completed. Usually, the fiscal calendar is the parameter for funding timetables.

The most difficult part about public funding is the paperwork and accountability involved. This paperwork begins with the grant proposal or letter of interest. This process takes time and energy due to the extensive nature of justification for resource allocation. The organization must provide quantitative, measurable performance related data showing why funds should be spent, how they benefit the taxpayer and how this will be accounted for. If not providing the particular service has the same results as performing the service, why would or should hard earned tax dollars be spent on the service?

Once the grant is secured, then the daily oversight and accountability begins. This is usually quite extensive and time consuming. Oversight is necessary because the large amount of corruption present in public funding. Having a person that is detail oriented and proficient with spread sheets, budgets and various forms is essential. Many government agencies have their own data collection software and electronic sites where information must be uploaded and preserved. This requires computer competence, training, and dedicated time just for the accountability portion of grant funding.

When a company receives government funding, they have expectations of what those funds will be used for. If those funds are used incorrectly the grant will stop, funds will cease and if corruption is present criminal charges will be pursued. Organizations must also make sure they do not receive funds for the same services from different groups. This is considered fraud, even when an organization does not understand what they have done is wrong. For example, if ministry X receives $100.00 from O County for employment services performed for John Smith, they cannot legally receive $50.00 from State Agency Y for the same services to Mr. Smith. Now ministry X may have incurred costs that exceed the $100.00 and they may have helped another individual that does not qualify for reimbursements, yet those costs must be covered in a different manner.

Public funding generally stipulates that funding cannot be utilized to proselytize or perform religious services of any sort. This is one of the difficult issues in a faith-based ministry. Often services that are funded must not have overly religious portions attached. For example, some groups have been given money for substance abuse programs. They are required to use a program like Alcoholics Anonymous but informed the funds would not cover the Celebrate Recovery Program. Faith based ministries must respect the stipulations of the funding they receive. This is why public funding may not be the best choice. Private supporters are not as reliable, yet the funds have fewer restrictions which free up time, energy, and complicated decision processes. The benefits and drawbacks of private funding will be discussed further in the next section.

BENEFITS AND DRAWBACKS OF PRIVATE FUNDING

Private funding is the way to go, if possible, yet private funding does not eliminate every problem. Private donations are just as difficult to receive as grants. If the private funding is from a Trust those funds will most likely come in the form of a designated offering, meaning the donor desires and expects the money to be spent on particular services. For example, if an organization is seeking funds for a new home or vehicle and they receive those funds the day before they realize there is a major roof leak in their primary building, they cannot arbitrarily decide to use the funds they received to perform the repairs. A best practice would be to honestly share the dilemma with the donor and ask if they would be okay with the funds being used instead for the newly discovered repair. Honesty and transparency are always the best policy. If donors do not feel that the organization can be trusted to do the right thing, they will find other groups to support.

When I served as a pastor, every week I received dozens of requests for funding. Most of the request came from great ministries and missionaries that were performing wonderful services to people in need. The problem was, we as a church already supported many different ministries and our resources were limited. There is always more ministry than money. One of the benefits of private funding is the ability to receive many small donations. Like a brick wall, each brick by itself, may be small but essential. If the ministry has a lot of small donations each month, they are less susceptible to financial problems when one donor stops support. In Song of Songs Chapter 2 it states that the little foxes ruin the vineyard. This is a negative connotation; however, the idea works in reverse as well. It is not one giant fox tearing things up, its many little creatures. A lot of something little does the job of a few things that are larger.

People give and stop giving for a myriad of reasons; some because they like or dislike what the ministry is focused upon at any given time. Some have personal budget issues; some stop giving to charity and start helping family in need. There are as many reasons as one can imagine. The financially wise in ministry will attempt to limit their vulnerability to shifts in giving. The biblically wise will keep a clear focus on the mission and make sure the organization's goals do not become watered down or curtailed to any particular donor. Be honest about the goals and needs of the group and if a potential donor does not want to support the work, allow them to walk away. This does not mean that you should never listen to advice or hear other's thoughts about improving the ministry, but make sure the goal is never set aside for the hope of maintaining a ministry that is ineffective.

WORK FORCE

The people serving in your organization—whether volunteer, staff, or board members—ideally will have a passion to help those who are often overlooked, marginalized and in need. This type of work does reduce crime, and prevent future victimization, but the people served are not the victims they are the ones who have been incarcerated. I recently spoke to a group of volunteers during an orientation/ training event and clearly told them that in this particular area of service you will be working with violent and nonviolent ex-offenders, some of the strongest Christians I know committed murder in their past. I instructed our group that if they could not accept this fact, then this is not the best area for them to serve. Being used by Christ to legitimately change lives is not always easy. Most of the time, we must be willing to step way out of our comfort zone in faith. This is the quality you want in people who serve in this type of ministry. Let us attempt to look at the primary areas of service in greater detail.

BOARD

The goal of the board is to help the president or executive director carryout services with as much ease as possible. They should also serve as an oversight group that ensures the wellbeing and security of the organization. It is always tricky and divisive to attempt to define a board or trustee's responsibility. However, I will provide my biased option.

For the director to carry out the work they must have as much freedom as possible. The director is the key subject matter expert, living in the trench day in and day out. This person understands what works, what needs to be avoided and the day-to-day drudgery of the ministry. This fact should afford them the freedom necessary for success.

The board comes in once a month or once a quarter and provides insight and advice for specific task. They should hopefully be comprised of experts in other fields that can aid in the work of the ministry. For example, having an accountant, a lawyer, a public media expert or a person with fund raising abilities can have their skills leveraged to improve the organization.

The board should also have the ability to see the financials, know what is occurring and speak to policies and procedures. They should not be the guiding force or steering the organization; however, they should ensure that the plan is being executed ethically, legally and with the best, long-term interest of the group.

It is always wise to attempt to have a board with varying back grounds and areas of knowledge. If your group is seeking public or private grants, the board will be evaluated. Grantors want to make sure their resources are going where they think they will be best used. If the board is diverse in professional background, this aids in funding.

One last, important issue with board members, it is wonderful to have board members that donate to the organization. And if they genuinely believe in the work, hopefully they will. But remember, just because a board member is a large donor, they should not be permitted to step into the power broker realm and abuse the ministry by pushing their agenda.

VOLUNTEERS

Volunteers are the life blood of nonprofits; they are how so much is accomplished with so little. Developing your volunteers is essential, utilizing your volunteers in the best way possible is also key to retaining them. Volunteers must have adequate time to rest and enjoy the benefits of the ministry.

Developing your volunteers can take many forms, from set aside times where instruction, guidance and education is provided to one-on-one meetings, maybe lunch or coffee where goals and insight into the organization is clarified. I served as a volunteer in many organizations, and nothing is more frustrating than working hard and finding out what you are doing is not a priority or even a desired goal of the group. Knowing what to do and how to do it keeps volunteers engaged and useful. From time to time a special retreat or weekend could be planned where experts come in and provide cultivation. This would also be great for team building.

The utilization of volunteers' piggy backs on this same concept. The volunteer may love the organization, want what is best for it and become frustrated and quit if they are not used in a meaningful way. This is tricky and often a hard line to delineate. Some volunteers only want to serve in a manner that they desire, sometimes their desires are not helpful to the organization. When I was a brand-new pastor, I had a church in an affluent neighborhood. Our church had been there over a hundred years, but the property values had skyrocketed and the people who had been present, started selling off their land and moving because relocating was such a profitable endeavor. Our church decided to collect food for the needy one thanksgiving, and I was assigned to deliver it to all the needy people in our neighborhood. This was in the year 2000, and the average home value in that area was over $350,000.00, the average income for a family was approximately $80-120,000.00. The only people I could think of that might need the food were the ones who helped collect it. They were the ones in the neighborhood before the massive influx of affluent residents. My point here is, if we have volunteers, they need task that have a purpose, we need to be able to articulate that purpose, equip them for that purpose and then allow them to serve.

The volunteer will be most effective over the long haul if they have adequate time to experience the fruit of the work. Meaning they must take volunteer sabbaticals. They must have times where they can decompress, participate in a program or service without the responsibilities of a volunteer.

In my personal experience I have found myself so engulfed in volunteering that I neglected self-care. This is especially dangerous when soul care is the primary goal of volunteering. Meaning if you are helping in say a church where guidance is being provided for spiritual cultivation and you never receive any of this assistance due to your amount of volunteer activity, you are doing self-harm. I have found myself sitting out of services and not going because I had been so busy. Even pastors need spiritual guidance, sermons, teaching, reproof, cultivation, and the sort. There is only one perfect being to ever walk this earth and it is not you or me.

PAID STAFF

Paid staff, just like board members and volunteers must have a passion for the work. If they lack the desire to serve in this type of ministry the kindest thing you can do is to free them up to work somewhere else. It is also the best and most protective action you can take for the ministry. If a person is simply working at a job for monetary compensation, they are not the best match.

Certainly, we have all had jobs we were not passionate about, but this is not a task where people should be spending time figuring out what their calling might be. They can explore that personal question as a volunteer. Working at a transition service is a difficult yet important, life changing endeavor.

Working at church, in the state prison system and later at the county jail, three issues were made clear regarding work. We must have the knowledge to carry out the job, we must then ascertain the skill for the task and lastly but most valuable, we must have the will to perform the task appropriately. We could ascribe almost any vocation to this concept. But for simplicity of point, let us think about this with something simple like painting a room. Let us say you are hired to be a painter. You show up and the "knowledge" portion of the job is clarified; you are told your task is to paint a particular room. Now you have the knowledge, next you need the skill. The foreman says we use paint brushes and rollers, not the spray gun, he picks up a roller, points at a paint can and quickly gives you a tutorial. Now, you have the beginnings of the skill set needed. This is great, you have the knowledge and skill to do your new job, but does that mean the room will get painted? Does that mean you will do a good job? Does that mean that once the boss walks away and is out of site, that you will not also leave? What must accompany knowledge and skill is will or desire to do the work and do it well.

The paid staff team must be passionate about the work and have a desire to carry out the task well, even when they are difficult. The team needs to be able to work cooperatively, communicate effectively and remember the key goal, which must be shared by all team members. This means that when conflict does occur, the team can remember that the key task, the main point of ministry is still at the core. This reminder helps bring conflict back to manageable disagreements that are focused best on how to do the key task.

The paid staff need to be able to do the task, so back to the skill concept, the staff should be equipped or come equipped to the job. Reentry and transition is a service where manipulation and deception go hand in hand. Our clients, many of which have spent decades inside the prison system say, "if a person does not know how to manipulate prior to going to prison, they sure know how once released." At least once a month, usually once a week, someone will reach out to our ministry and state that they also want to help ex-offenders, they also want to possibly provide housing and other needs. This is a noble desire, there are more people being released everyday than there are reentry centers to help. However, if the good-hearted person who wants to help has no knowledge and experience working with this population, they should gain that first, prior to establishing a center or ministry where people could get hurt. We often encourage ministry minded people to volunteer at our program, a program like ours or at the Department of Corrections. This enables the person to serve in a real-life situation where people benefit and for them to better understand what they hope to do in ministry.

RESIDENTIAL SERVICES

In Chapter 1. Section B. *How the purpose is exercised*, we looked at the logistics of how a person approaches this ministry with residential needs. We do not need to advertise; we receive more letters requesting services a week that we have room for in months. Our staff does make our services known when we have opportunity to speak in the local jail and state prison, but the incarcerated population share information, and we currently receive letters from every State correctional facility in Florida, many other states, and federal facilities as well.

There are a few things we do purposefully because we have learned lessons the hard way and sharing them here will hopefully help others avoid our mistakes. To begin with we choose to use houses over larger facilities like a hotel or apartment complexes. This may sound odd, logistically, and financially it seems like it would make more sense to have one location, one property to maintain and one site where all the clients were gathered. The reality is different due to real life practical implications, lets investigate this further.

WHY HOUSES

We purposefully use houses for several reasons. Single family houses are an easy way for the clients to experience a family style environment. They are required to cooperate with use of the amenities. They have to learn how to share the bathroom, washer and dryer, cooking responsibilities and other common spaces. This exercise is something that many of the men have never learned or experienced, depending on their upbringing. The house, located in a normal neighborhood provides a sense of real life, true trust, and acclimation back to society.

Next, we use the single-family environment because we occasionally have a person who relapses. When this takes place, it is often accompanied by a second and sometimes third client relapsing. 1 Corinthians 15:33 (KJV), "Do not be misled: 'Bad company corrupts good character.'" We have had to shut down a house, relocate all clients and even remove clients from the program. This is much easier and results in fewer clients becoming affected if there is some separation. If we had a converted hotel with twenty-five clients and a large portion started using drugs it would be difficult to identify, correct, and isolate the issue.

Working with large groups increases the likelihood of bedbugs, illness, or other unwanted problems. We have had to treat houses for bed bugs on multiple occasions. Treating a thirteen hundred square foot, three-bedroom, two-bathroom home is much easier and cost less than treating a hotel. In Florida, ADA and fire codes must also be adhered to in larger facilities. These restrictions can be expensive when employed in large environments.

Individual houses allow us the opportunity to expand our services or decrease our footprint by simply purchasing or selling a single home. If we have greater need and resources, we can quicky add a house location, instead of relocating to a larger facility.

RESPONSIBILITIES/EXPECTATIONS

The responsibilities and expectations for the individual residential client are at the core simple, we desire a genuine, real, and authentic client striving for what is best. We experience as many different challenges as we have clients. We do have standard rules for each house. We have curfews, rules about alcohol, visitors, and cleanliness, however, each person experiences grace in our program.

Every person is trying to figure out their transition based off past life experiences and what they are currently learning in our program. Some of these guys had horrible upbringings and have spent their entire adult life behind bars. Some of them have never developed good decision-making skills. Most of us made vocational and relational mistakes at sixteen, seventeen and eighteen. Many of the clients, even though they may be thirty, are still locked in the late teens mind frame, because that is where they were when incarcerated.

This is where experience, time spent with the men, and time spent with God makes the difference. Godly discernment is key. But unfortunately, we do not always listen as we should to the Holy Spirit or naively think we must be misunderstanding his directing because it appears contradictory to the love and mercy, we see in the Bible.

Sometimes we must make hard decisions and remove men from our program.

This is never easy but for the safety of the other clients and to mitigate the risk to the ministry and safeguard its longevity we must stop people from causing damage. This is ideally performed with other options and resources presented as they are informed of their removal. If we identify that an individual has repeatedly and habitually broke the alcohol policy, we try to help them secure a spot at an alcohol rehabilitation treatment center. I said ideally because this is seldom how the meetings with the clients play out. There is usually hostility and anger at being re-moved from the program, even though the choices were performed by the client that led to the removal.

Trusting that God is all powerful and nothing happens outside of his knowledge is important to grasp as you perform these difficult tasks. Knowing that prison can be a form of grace and that spiritual maturity and even salvation can come through trials, is helpful when performing these hard sections of residential services.

There are two main theories I have witnesses when it comes to expectations of residential clients. I know some programs keep the clients so busy that they do not have time to make mistakes. They keep them occupied from dusk till dawn with labor and isolate them from any outside temptations. I think this is exactly what some people need. However, in our program we are attempting to prepare the client for a self-sustaining, productive, flourishing life. This comes from much self-discipline and feeding of the new nature, incrementally, so they can mature into what God has designed for them. The positive outcome is seldom an easy path, but it is absolutely attainable, we have many success stories.

SECONDARY GOAL: A BETTER, SAFER LIFE FOR ALL CITIZENS

Reentry and Transition of ex-offenders back into society is not near as volatile a subject as it once was. Matter of fact, it has become much more supported and recognized for its benefits than probably ever before in history. This is because the positive results are more visible now than ever before, more organizations are keeping quantitative data, the Departments of Corrections in most states also have numeric metrics that evidence the good provided by groups endeavoring to assist those returning.

The data shows that the person who committed the crime is helped, but society also benefits from the interruption of recidivism and victimization. Successful reentry and transition endeavors help people not to reoffend. This equates to fewer crimes, fewer victims, less court cost, less incarceration expenses that result in less tax dollars being spent and less emotional damage to victims, their family and the family of the person involved in the crime.

This is the strange paradigm of reentry and transition. Most people heavily lean one way or the other. They like the services because they feel strongly about restorative justice.

They want people to experience a true second chance and understand many offenders had horrible upbringings and the cards were stacked against them from the start. Others like transition because it provides a safer environment for them to live and raise a family. If each city across the United States has people returning from prison each year, you do not want them coming to your city unless they have changed. I also share the desire for my family to remain safe, I do not want them to ever be victimized.

When I speak with potential supporters of reentry and transition, I generally focus on one of these sides of service, the restorative side, or the lower crime side. Both are true; people are restored, and crime is lessened. This is a ministry and process that is positive for everyone.

EMPLOYMENT SERVICES

Securing meaningful employment is essential in breaking the cycle. Employment provides many of the desires people have, even in the Garden of Eden, before the fall, work was part of God's plan. Working, paying bills, purchasing things that are desired without relying on another person's charity encourages confidence and self-worth. Keeping busy at a job also keeps individuals away from endeavors that have a propensity to be illegal or at minimum less than helpful.

FIND A JOB, AND FIND ANOTHER JOB

The dilemma faced by most individuals returning from prison is not employment, its meaningful, lasting, and sufficient employment. North Florida is a forgiving area, with plenty of employment opportunities, however many of the jobs require personal transportation. Some cities do not offer public transportation at all. Even though busses are available, it is not abnormal for our new clients to spend 4-6 hours a day getting back and forth from work, if relying on public transportation. We intentionally keep houses on bus routes, but being a city that is spread out geographically, the bus can make many stops and traverse almost the entire city before it carries them to their work or back home.

Most of our new clients secure a job, that helps meet basic needs while they work toward securing transportation to enable them to pursue the forever job they wish to acquire. Knowing that most return to society with on average between $2,000 and $5,000.00 of court cost, restitution, back child support, alimony, probation fees etc. Finding that first job, even if it is not great, is a step in the right direction.

Our employment specialist keeps these challenges in mind when helping to secure that first job. We strive to assist in the first, second, and even third job if needed. Matter of fact, I know that one of our employment specialists has helped an individual over the last two years secure over ten jobs.

We try to get the person placed quickly and then look for the forever job that takes longer to secure. Much of our funding is performance based, meaning that we only receive reimbursement for one time if the client qualifies. Therefore, every time we assist in finding a second, third, or even tenth job, it is pro-bono. However, that is why we exist—to help people—and that is why private funding is so valuable.

FOLLOW UP

We do write to persons that have identified they are returning to Duval County after release from prison, but most of our clients for employment and all of our residential clients hear about us through what is called on the inside as "Inmate.com" (meaning *word of mouth*). A good reputation is important. Our staff care about the ministry and care about the clients. This is why we try to follow up and see how the clients are doing.

This is easy with residential clients but much harder with the employment clientele. We desire to know how the job is going, we rely on feedback to determine best practices and how we can continue to improve.

PROGRAMS

"Programs" is the word we use to describe all our cultivating and character development initiatives. This is an area that is constantly needing evaluation, modification, and attention. The classes, meetings and groups used in this endeavor will change with the individuals present if it is being performed properly. No two people and no two groups of people will have the same needs. There certainly are similarities and overriding key issues yet how to provide the needed help in the best way possible will alter from person to person.

As mentioned earlier, we strive to change the heart through a genuine relationship with Jesus Christ. We attempt to present Jesus in an evangelistic manner without proselytizing people. This simply means, we do not manipulate of force conversion in any way. However, knowing that only a life surrendered to Christ can experience a flourishing existence we utilize Godly principles in all of our character development initiatives. Below are a few areas of focus that help the clients adjust in a healthy way back into society.

SUBSTANCE ABUSE

This may be a generalization, yet it is usually true, most of our clients have some type of substance abuse issue. If you look at an arrest sheet and the person has had several B&E, breaking and entering or petty theft charges, they usually are stealing to pay for drugs. Many people, who are not intimately familiar with the prison system think that if a person is incarcerated, they are not using drugs or alcohol during their time inside. That is simply not true, just like in free society, the individual must make a choice to avoid temptations while inside prison as well. All types of vices are available in prison and if an addict does not get the help they need while incarcerated they will leave prison no better off than when they entered.

The substance abuse program offered must be practical in nature, providing real life advice and help to people who know and understand how to manipulate to get what they want. It must be on a level that is understandable and the absolute best way for it to be successful is for the accountability and guidance to come from those who have experienced the same dilemmas in the past. We will speak more about this in the Life skills section when we address the need for alumni to be engaged.

MENTORING

Mentoring is a wonderful tool, where relationships are developed. At least once a month we meet formally for a time of mentorship. Proverbs 27:17(KJV), "Iron sharpeneth iron; so a man sharpeneth the countenance of his friend" The clients are asked to prepare for the meeting by reading a study guide, then asked several open-ended questions to help motivate conversation. The curriculum is valuable, and we have used several different types, however the goal is to develop a genuine relationship between a mature individual and a person just returning from incarceration. The goal is for our clients to have an additional source to receive good advice, godly wisdom, and guidance. We are not at all upset when the conversations move from the curriculum to questions about relationships, starting a bank account or interpersonal conflicts at work. We hope they receive advice from true leaders instead of old acquaintances.

We also encourage them to talk more than once a month, to text or call each other. However, we do promote several safety stops for this relationship. We clearly inform both client and mentors that there should never be a time when they are at each other's residence, there should never be a time of borrowing money and that at any time a client or mentor feels uncomfortable they should call our staff immediately. Our volunteers are background screened and are also required to read and sign the most current PREA (Prison Rape Elimination Act) information from the Florida Department of Corrections. We hope for the best but want to be prepared for the worst.

LIFE SKILLS

The life skills portion of our programs consist of budgeting courses, anger management, workplace etiquette and most importantly the alumni seminars. We have been in operation since 1990 and in that time, we have had many wonderful success stories. The absolute best thing we do after sharing Christ is having people who went through the program, who are thriving in society come and share their story.

They have insight and real-life experience that cannot be duplicated in an academic fashion; no curriculum can provide what they learned the hard way. They have the credibility required for many of the clients to truly listen. This is the night of the month, no one should miss. The alumni often share about their upbringing, first crimes, the event that landed them in prison and then the struggle from then on. Many of the successful clients spent several decades behind bars. Some up to forty years. They also share about their first job, the struggle to get to and from, the adjustment back to a society that had drastically altered while they were gone. Then they speak about the personal, family relationships that have been fractured and how they have worked to mend them.

The individuals who have recently been released need to hear from people who have felt just as they feel. Guys who have stayed in the house they stay, walked the same road, and struggled to find adequate transportation to work. They need to know success is possible, not easy, but possible. They also need to hear from the men how they slipped at times, how temptation is always present and how they must seek help when needed.

We are blessed to have several alumni who come and mentor also. We also have many alumni who give financially to POC each month. This is a blessing and confirmation that we are on the right path. Many of the POC alumni also go back into the prisons on a regular basis to encourage, share and mentor inside, they meet with at risk youth and help in many churches. These are people who committed a crime, some of them committed murder, but they are new in Christ and go above and beyond to help others.

CHARACTER DEVELOPMENT

Character development is an everyday endeavor with our clients. I would say it is also an everyday endeavor with our staff also. We want to be and do the best we can, yet this is a work that often pulls the curtain back from society and allows you to peek inside and see the worst. Recently my daughter told me a disturbing story she heard about a workplace associate who was assaulted. She said, "Dad isn't that the worst thing you have ever heard?" I paused for a second and simply said that is a terrible occurrence. The truth is, that did not even rank in the top ten worst things I have heard or seen. I worked Death Row, and I have been a deputy with a county sheriff's office. The things I have witnessed are pretty bad. I cannot imagine what war time veterans have seen. This all confirms the truth of the Bible, that we are sinful people living on a cursed earth and in desperate need of a rescuer.

The point I am attempting to make is, if we are not close to God, we will become disillusioned with what we view every day and become callous. Last summer my wife and I were driving and came upon a fatality scene, a bicycler had been struck by a car and the first responders who had been there a while were not near as upset as my wife at what she saw. She looked at me and said, "are they joking around?" I quickly said honey, they are just as disturbed as you, however this is not an unusual site for them, they deal with this every day. Part of what you witnessed was them coping with the dark side of life.

My wife was right, that they were not showing the proper respect, any non-first responder would have been shocked by their demeanor, however, after serving in a role where disturbing events occur every hour. I know there must be times when somebody lightens the mood. This does not grant permission for disrespect or any form of degradation. It is also not permission to sin and disconnect from humanity.

When I first went to work in the prison, it was common practice to refer to the incarcerated population simply as "inmate." This was much more than attempting to get the attention of a person in which you might not remember their name. It was a form of separating them from dignity and humanity. It depersonalized the individual. It allowed the officer to not get close or attached to a person, but to view the other person as a task, job, or product. Most prisons today are referred to as "Correctional Institutions," this change in verbiage was derived from a change in ideology, society believes people are being reformed or "Corrected." If de humanization is occurring how on earth is a person being lifted up and prepared for after incarceration? Ex-Offenders are now being referred to as "Returning Citizens" and Sexual Offenders are being called "Registered Citizens." This is an effort to restore dignity, however there is some confusion and few people, at this time understand the new language, only time will tell if it becomes permanent.

On a lesser level, people do this in most jobs, even pastors can find themselves focusing on outcome instead of people. We must stay mentally and spiritually well to perform difficult task like ministry. It is easy to lose sight of the goal which is people.

If you are a ministry leader, character growth must be occurring before you can expect or assist your clients to mature. We must remain teachable, constantly striving to learn, grow and expand, or there is no way an onlooker will say, "Hey, I want what they have."

PARTNERS

Partnerships in ministry are important. There is always more work than any one group can perform, and working with similar ministries helps the people you serve. Partnering with groups that differ from your ministry help both groups assist people in ways they themselves are not equipped to assist. It is important to remember that you are not in competition with other organizations. Some of the most valuable blessings we have experienced have been from other nonprofit entities that are also striving to help people. We should always look for ways to lift each other up and serve each other in ways we can.

I have personally reaped the benefits of serving at a ministry with a long reputation of cooperation. The last several times I have spoken in public where other ministries were also able to share, several of the other groups bragged about us and our willingness to always help. A good reputation goes so much further than advertising and self-promotion.

FORMAL COOPERATION

Formal cooperation is when you are in contract with or operate under an (MOU), (MOA) memorandum of understanding or memorandum of agreement. These are written agreed upon terms of operation and cooperation. All public grants will use these written, legal documents. This is a way to protect both parties and assure what has been promised is what will be performed.

Formal cooperation clarifies expectations for both parties and eliminates confusion. This does not mean everything is perfect and a formal agreement does not mean there is a lack of trust by either party. They simply provide another layer of accountability. Formal, written, legally binding documentation is a great safety net for community-based organizations (CBO).

If a small nonprofit has a particular focus of service and have been promised support for that service only to have that support pulled mid service it can sink them, financially. They have to choose to stop helping the people being served or go out of business. A formal agreement holds both parties accountable ensuring that the service by the CBO is performed adequately while also guaranteeing that the promised support occurs.

INFORMAL COOPERATION

Informal cooperation should take place all the time, as mentioned earlier we should do our best to work with others. Our group also speaks in many prisons about reentry and transition. The state prison system invites us often. While at these seminars we network with other groups from around Florida and attempt to develop and strengthen our relationships. Not every person being released is coming back to our city, so it is a wonderful benefit to direct them to a good service in the location to which they are returning. They also go back to their dorm and pass the word that we care enough to help, even when we are not directly involved. Again, a good reputation is a blessing.

Informal cooperation also takes place in conversations where information is shared. I do not have any problem helping others know what I know. This is part of the reason for this writing. There is a genuine need in society for successful reentry services. If what we have learned in over thirty years can help others avoid heartache and mistakes, let's make that happen.

Other organizations will be much more willing to help you when they know you are willing to help them. Remember this is not a competition, this is a ministry, a service to help people, all people.

CONCLUSION

This small document was written for several reasons and hopefully they will all be accomplished. Most importantly I want to re affirm what was stated in chapter 1. The heart must change. That change only occurs when a person recognizes their powerlessness and inability to save/ help oneself. We must understand our state in God's eyes is that of a sinner. We must repent of that sin, turn from, and ask Christ to forgive us, we must also ask Him to provide the grace and power we need to live the life God desires for us. This need is for all people, the person who is sitting on death row and the person sitting in the oval office. All have sinned and fallen short of the Glory of God, but if we repent and seek forgiveness, He is faithful and just and will forgive us of all sins. I hope and pray that you have come to this point in your life. This is the only thing that will make a lasting difference for the people we hope to help.

Next, I hope this writing provides very real, practical advice and assistance, as you seek to serve or develop a ministry. Many of the concepts in this book transcend well into other ministries and nonprofit work. Some of the same dilemmas are present in any organization.

Lastly, I hope this booklet allows you to understand the work Prisoners of Christ is accomplishing. I invite you to partner with us financially. During my tenure as the

CEO/President of this great ministry I hope to develop a foundation that will ensure this ministry is fiscally stable for years to come.

We hustle every year to acquire grants, private donations and operate within a lean budget. Any donations that arise from this writing will be placed in a foundational trust where the interest helps offset operating cost each year. Your help will make an eternal difference in many lives. Those being released from prison will experience a true second chance and the community will experience fewer crimes.

If we could secure operational cost for our North Florida location, expansion into other areas would be much easier. If financial assistance was derived from private funding instead of public grants, the copious amounts of time spent on the grant process and continuing upkeep could be utilized in true ministry endeavors. Please pray about making a foundational gift.

Gifts may be directly given through our website, **www. pocjax.org**, or mailed to our office:

6940 Atlantic Blvd.
Jacksonville, FL 32211

Please specify this is a "foundational gift."

ABOUT THE AUTHOR

Jeff has ministered in Jacksonville and St. Johns County for many years. He was the senior pastor of Palm Valley Baptist Church in Ponte Vedra Beach Florida, where he served for fourteen years. He worked at The Florida State Prison "Raiford" on Death Row, and at Nassau County Sheriff's Office as a Classification Deputy. He currently serves as the President/CEO of Prisoners of Christ, Re-entry and Transition Service. He is also a certified private investigator and frequently testifies as an expert witness in the areas of post release, classification, and prison/jail procedures.

Jeff holds an undergraduate Divinity Degree from The Baptist College of Florida, a B.A. in Philosophy with a concentration in Applied Ethics from The University of North Florida and a Master of Public Administration Degree.

Jeff and his wife, Abby, have been married over twenty-five years and are the proud parents of two daughters.

CPSIA information can be obtained
at www.ICGtesting.com
Printed in the USA
LVHW052256181221
706603LV00004B/19